Rogue Robot

Written by John Parsons
Illustrated by Lloyd Foye

Contents	Page
Chapter 1. *Too many jobs to do*	4
Chapter 2. *The delivery*	8
Chapter 3. *Boris gets busy*	12
Chapter 4. *It's madness!*	22
Chapter 5. *We need a plan*	26
Chapter 6. *Useful after all!*	30
Verse	32

Rigby

Rogue Robot

With these characters ...

Mom & Dad

Me

Bouncer

Boris

"We were jus

Setting the scene ...

Ever wondered what it would be like to have a robot to do all your chores around the house? Well, it might not be too long before someone invents a robot that will do just that! But like all technology, things can go wrong—and having a weird robot running around your house might not be as much fun as you think.

A peek into this crazy story tells us that having chores to do is not so bad after all!

n ordinary family ..."

Chapter 1.

We were just an ordinary family, living in an ordinary house, on an ordinary street. Our troubles began one Saturday night when we were all sitting down to dinner.

"I'm exhausted," said my dad. "I've had to mow the lawn, sweep the sidewalk, go to the grocery store, and return the videos. I have too many jobs to do."

"You have too many jobs?" said my mom. "What about me? I had to do the washing, vacuum the house, clean the car, and change three light bulbs! I feel extremely weary."

I didn't want to be left out.

"I'm tired, too," I said. "I've got mountains of homework. I have to help clean the house *and* take Bouncer for walks and feed him every morning and evening. I don't have any energy left!"

We sat in front of the television, too tired to talk anymore. That's when the advertisement came on, and that was the moment we stopped being an ordinary family. Mom looked up from her newspaper. Dad put down his novel. I concentrated on the television screen. It was just what we needed.

"Get your very own robot!" said the advertisement. "Your personal robot can do all the chores that take up too much of your time. Your personal robot can leave you free to enjoy life! Buy one now! Our operators are standing by."

Before I knew it, Dad got out his credit card and called the robot company. Our own personal robot was going to be delivered tomorrow! We would be the first family on the block to have a robot. Our lives would be changed forever!

Chapter 2.

The next afternoon, we all stood around the front door when the delivery truck arrived.

We proudly carried the heavy cartons into the living room. Mom got out the assembly instructions.

"Now, just do as I say," she warned Dad. "I know what you are like around technology. It took you hours to connect the new videotape recorder last month!"

Actually, the instructions were fairly easy. By dinnertime, we had assembled our robot, and we had only a few parts left over.

"I don't know what they are for," said Dad. "They always put extra spare parts in these self-assembly things." Mom and I rolled our eyes.

"Sure, Dad," I said, grinning.

The last instruction said that we should charge up our robot overnight, so we plugged it in. We watched as the small red power light on the front of our robot grew bigger and brighter.

"What shall we call it?" asked Mom. "We have to have a name for our robot."

We all suggested a few names until Dad came up with a good one: Boris. So Boris it was. Boris, our personal robot. In our beds that night, we dreamed of all the jobs Boris would do for us. Best of all, we knew we could sleep in, because we'd have no jobs to do. How wrong we were!

Chapter 3.

It seemed like it was still the middle of the night when I was woken by a piercing, loud screaming sound. I leaped out of bed and ran for the light switch. As I raced across the room, I crashed into something metal and fell flat on my face.

I crawled to the light switch and turned it on. There, in the middle of my room, was Boris, fully charged and ready to go.

"WAKE UP CALL," he boomed. "Wake up!"

"Boris, it's four o'clock in the morning," I groaned, looking at my alarm clock. "What are you doing?"

"My calculations show you will have *more* time to relax if you get up NOW," ordered Boris. "Get ready now, and you can do nothing for even longer."

I screwed up my face. I began to wonder if I would like Boris quite as much as the ad said I would. This was not a good start.

I started to climb back into bed. In a flash, Boris pulled all the sheets, the blankets, the pillows, and the bedspread off my bed. He bundled everything up in his arms.

"This is the dirtiest bedspread I've ever seen!" said Boris. "I will wash everything *now*."

I staggered down the hallway and was about to go and wake up my parents. But Boris pushed past me. Before I could stop him, his siren started screaming in their bedroom. Dad just about hit the roof. Mom thought it was a fire alarm. She tried to crawl out the window, but Boris pulled her back.

"No time for that," he insisted. "Get dressed. Breakfast will be ready in a flash."

We sat on the edge of the bed, with stunned looks on our faces.

"Are you sure you read those instructions correctly?" Dad asked Mom. Mom gave Dad a very strange look.

"Are you sure about those extra spare parts?" she asked Dad.

Before he could answer, a roaring noise came from the kitchen. A huge ball of smoke burst down the hallway. Boris came whirring down the hall, carrying bowls of a black, soupy-looking mixture.

"What's that?" asked Mom, although I don't think she really wanted to know.

"Breakfast, of course," said Boris. "Eggs, toast, coffee, fruit, and cereal! They're all mixed together and mashed into sludge to save you time chewing. Then I cooked it all at three thousand degrees for ten seconds. Much quicker than the old-fashioned method," he added helpfully. "Eat NOW!"

We took our bowls and looked suspiciously at the burned sludge.

"I don't think we're very hungry," said Dad.

"Excellent," said Boris. "That will save even more time."

Suddenly, an enormous jet of soapy water gushed out of one of Boris's fingers and soaked us. Everyone was so surprised that we just stood there, dripping water all over the carpet. Then a huge blast of hot air from his other finger almost gave us instant sunburn.

"You are washed and dried," said Boris proudly. "Now you can go and relax."

"I guess we're lucky we didn't get dried off at three thousand degrees," I whispered to Mom.

"What was that?" asked Boris. "Are you too cold?"

"No, no, no!" we all shouted together. "We're just fine, thanks."

Boris bustled us all down the hallway and out the front door. It slammed behind us.

"Enjoy *all* your free time," came the robotic voice through the door. We heard a whirring sound as he shuffled down the hallway to do the housework.

There we were, in the dark, outside our house. Blow-dried and hungry at a quarter past four in the morning. I pinched myself. Surely, this was just a bad dream. I was sure that I was going to wake up and it was going to be nine-thirty. Boris would be happily and quietly whirring down the hall, bringing me some orange juice, scrambled eggs, and pancakes.

No matter how hard I pinched myself, the result was the same. This was for real! This was *not* a bad dream!

Chapter 4.

We went and sat in the car until sunrise. Mom kept nudging Dad in the ribs.

"Please go and see what *your* robot is destroying now!" she kept saying with a frown on her face.

"*My* robot?" said Dad, who was trying out his own strange frown on Mom. "I only followed *your* instructions."

"Hmm," said Mom. I don't think she was very impressed with Dad's knowledge of technology.

In the end, we all sneaked out of the car and crept up to the kitchen window. We peeked through the window and gasped in horror.

The robot was whirling around, rearranging all the furniture. It was stripping the wallpaper off the walls, lifting up the carpet, and hosing everything down with an enormously powerful jet of water.

I noticed my dog, Bouncer, shivering behind one of the chairs, looking extremely worried. At the same time, so did Boris.

"WALKIES!" shouted the crazy robot. A long chain sprang out from his middle, and he clipped it around Bouncer's collar. Poor Bouncer! Boris marched off down the hallway, dragging Bouncer behind him. The front door slammed, and Boris raced down the street at about sixty miles an hour. All I could see of Bouncer was a brown blur with an outstretched tail. I don't know if the dog was running or bouncing, but I was willing to bet he wasn't going to be wanting two walks today!

We took the opportunity to sneak into the house, grab some food and drinks from the kitchen, and hide ourselves in the living room. Just to be sure we wouldn't be found, Mom and Dad piled up the couch and chairs against the door. We didn't want our crazy personal robot checking to see just how *much* we were relaxing. We had to work out a plan to stop Boris quickly, before we all became as crazy as he was!

Chapter 5.

By nightfall, we could only imagine what was happening outside our safe living room. We guessed that whatever it was, it would be time-saving and completely disastrous. The only time we dared to check Boris was when we could peek through the window. He was setting the back lawn on fire with his powerful flamethrower.

"No more grass. No more lawn mowing," he announced cheerfully. "We'll save hours and hours every week," he added, and off he zoomed.

Dad slumped onto the couch and pulled a cushion over his head. Lucky he did, because I think Mom was about to throw the other one at him anyway.

Eventually, there was a soft knock at the door.

"Excuse me, happy family," came Boris's eager voice. "It's nighttime. I need to be recharged for the morning. Please plug in my power cord."

"You need to be recharged?" asked Dad suspiciously.

"Oh, yes," said Boris. "Someone left out my self-charging unit when I was assembled. So I need recharging. NOW."

"Just a minute," said Dad. He smiled at Mom. "And you thought I just left those parts out by mistake," he smiled. Mom just rolled her eyes.

Now we had the plan we'd been hoping for!

We moved all the furniture away from the door and slowly opened it. The red light on Boris was getting very dim, and it flickered every few seconds.

"Please plug in my power cord," he said in a very low voice. "Please plug in my power cord."

His voice almost faded out. Dad whipped around behind Boris and tipped him over. I grabbed his wheels and quickly unscrewed them from the sockets. Mom wrenched off both arms. Boris was defenseless and unable to move. At last, we were back in control of our house. We all breathed a sigh of relief.

Mom and Dad went out to survey the damage, and I settled down in front of the computer to do my homework. Bouncer flopped, exhausted, by my side. At last, everything was peaceful. At last, everything was back to normal.

Chapter 6.

There I was, trying to figure out some really hard math problems, when I heard a soft whirring sound behind me.

"That looks easy," said a very faint voice. "I can solve all those math problems in three minutes."

I turned to see a faint red glow flickering in Boris's light.

Bouncer looked frightened and whimpered, but I just smiled. I tugged Boris (*without* his wheels and arms) into my bedroom. I plugged in his power cord and put him in front of the computer.

Boris *was* going to be useful, after all.

"We were just an ordinary family ..."

Reprogrammed and
Out of control
Bodies of steel
Out on the loose
Talking and listening
Secretly planning.